A Rainy Day for Sammy

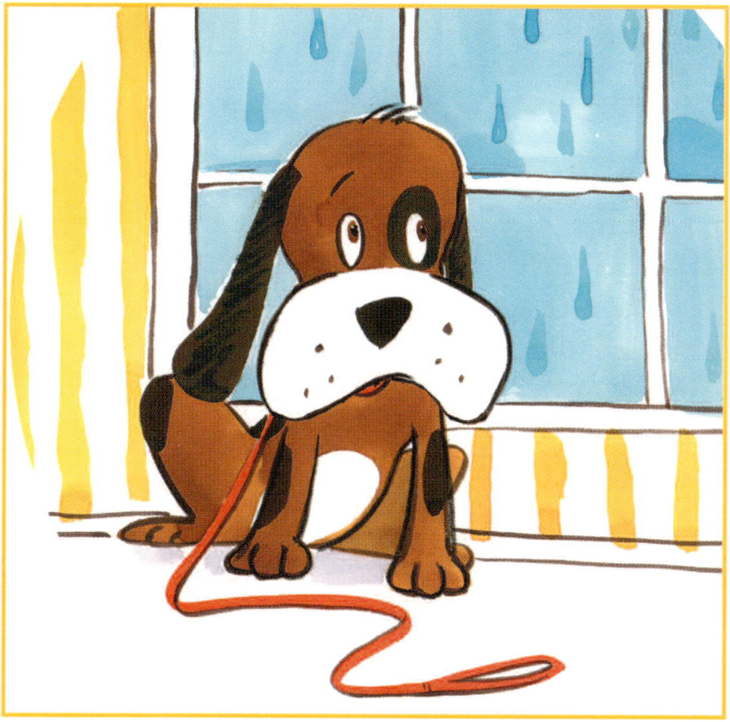

written by Kathleen Urmston and Grant Urmston
illustrated by Gloria Gedeon

KAEDEN BOOKS™

The house was very quiet.
No one was home. Suddenly
the back door opened with
a squeak.

Sammy opened his eyes and waited.

The back door closed. The book bag dropped to the floor.

Hi, Sammy.
I'm home.
Let's go out.

Sammy stood up, yawned and stretched his legs.

Sammy slowly moved toward the door.

Sammy saw the rain.

"Come on, Sammy. Let's go out. Let me put on your leash."

Sammy did not want to go out in the rain.

Sammy ran around the table and ran out of the kitchen. Grant ran after him.

"Sammy, let's go out," called Grant.

Sammy ran through the dining room,

up the stairs, down the stairs,

into the living room, past the den,

into the family room, and around the chair.

Panting, Sammy stopped to rest.
Grant rested too.

"OK, Sammy, you've had enough fun," said Grant. "Let's go outside. Here is your leash."

Sammy took off running again.

Sammy ran around the kitchen table,

into the dining room, through the living room,

up the stairs,

over the bed,

down the stairs, toward the kitchen.

Sammy heard something. He tried to stop but he was running too fast.

Mom heard barking as she came into the kitchen and put the groceries on the floor.

Just then, Sammy rounded the corner and . . .

Sammy ran into the grocery bags. Food went everywhere! "Uh-oh! Time for another bath!" said Mom.